WORKBOOK FOR

CALM YOUR MIND WITH FOOD

(A Guide to Uma Naidoo's Book)

We wish you the best of
luck and hope that this
book helps you achieve
your goals.

NOW IS THE TIME TO CHECK OUT THE TOP TIPS FOR BEING SUCCESSFUL IN USING THIS BOOK.

➢ Realize before you go any further that lying to yourself is among the worst things you can do. While following this guide, be honest with yourself.

➢ Use this guidance with caution and thoroughness while you seek out a guardian. It

must be an accountable
individual.

➢ Engrave the book's
teachings and principles
deeply into your mind. It
needs to permeate your
entire being.

➢ When you get to the
notes section, really let
your thoughts flow.

➢ It is not an illusion;
everything is actually
feasible here.

BEGINNING THE PROCESS OF CHANGE

A STATE OF MIND THAT COULD TRANSFORM

Activities that promote self-care may alleviate stress and anxiety. Exercise and mindfulness are examples.

<u>Practical Steps You Can Do Right Now</u>

Many experience daily stress. Daily stressors include work, family, health, and finances.

DIFFICULTY WITH PERPETUAL

THOUGHT

Minimizing everyday
chronic stress may
improve your health.
Chronic stress increases
heart disease, anxiety,
and depression risk.

Everything that is been occupying your thoughts

Regular exercise may
relieve stress and
enhance happiness.

A 6-week study of 185 university students revealed that aerobic exercise twice a week lowered overall and uncertainty-related stress.

Moreover, the exercise
practice was shown to
considerably alleviate
the individual's self-
reported depression.

FINAL ARTICLE!

Regular exercise improves
symptoms. Reliable source
for anxiety and
depression.

A STATE OF MIND THAT
COULD TRANSFORM

Inactive people should
start with mild exercises
like walking or riding.
Picking an exercise you
like may help you keep
with it.

Practical Steps You Can Do Right Now

Each and every facet of your health, including your mental health, is influenced by the food that you consume.

DIFFICULTY WITH PERPETUAL

THOUGHT

A 2022 analysis found
that ultra-processed and
sugary diets increase
subjective stress.

Everything that is been occupying your thoughts

If you're constantly worried, you might eat too much and choose foods that taste great, which is bad for your health and happiness.

Not eating enough
nutrient-dense whole
foods may lead to
magnesium and B vitamin
deficits, which regulate
stress and mood.

Reduce your consumption of processed meals and drinks and consume more real foods to fuel your body.

FINAL ARTICLE!

Smartphones, computers, and apps are useful sometimes, but using them too much may make you feel more stressed.

IT IS THE THIRD DAY OF YOUR TRANSFORMATION

A STATE OF MIND THAT COULD TRANSFORM

A review of the literature from 2021 says that several studies have found a link between using your phone too much and mental health problems and higher amounts of stress.

<u>Practical Steps You Can Do Right Now</u>

Being mentally and emotionally unhealthy and having more stress are both linked to spending too much time in front of screens.

DIFFICULTY WITH PERPETUAL

THOUGHT

Also, spending too much
time in front of a screen
may make it harder to
sleep, which can make you
feel more stressed.

EVERYTHING THAT IS BEEN

OCCUPYING YOUR THOUGHTS

It is possible that reducing your stress levels might be accomplished by setting aside time to engage in self-care activities.

Self-care reduces stress and improves quality of life, whereas neglecting it increases tension and burnout.

Self-care is vital for
wellness. Nurses,
physicians, teachers, and
caregivers are extremely
stressed, thus this is
crucial.

FINAL ARTICLE!

Taking care of yourself
doesn't have to be hard
or difficult. It just
means taking care of your
health and happiness.

FOURTH DAY OF YOUR
TRANSFORMATION

A STATE OF MIND THAT
COULD TRANSFORM

Being exposed to certain
aromas, such as those
found in candles or
essential oils, may be
particularly relaxing.

Practical Steps You Can Do Right Now

It is referred to as
aromatherapy when you use
smells to improve your
mood. Aromatherapy has
been shown to reduce

anxiety and improve sleep
quality.

DIFFICULTY WITH PERPETUAL

THOUGHT

Keeping a journal can
help you deal with your
feelings and thoughts in

a healthy way, which may help lower your worry and anxiety.

Everything that is been occupying your thoughts

Expressive or therapeutic writing may help patients with chronic health disorders, including depression, according to a 2018 research.

Regular writing may
improve quality of life,
self-care, and healthier
habits like taking
prescriptions.

Caffeine is a drug that makes you feel more alert. It's found in coffee, tea, chocolate, and energy drinks.

FINAL ARTICLE!

A 2021 study of the literature on the subject

found that eating too
much may make worry
worse.

This is Day 5 of Your
Transformation

A STATE OF MIND THAT COULD TRANSFORM

Too much may also make it
hard to sleep. In turn,

this may make worry and
nervousness worse.

Practical Steps You Can Do Right Now

Individuals have varying
limits of tolerance when
it comes to the amount of
caffeine they can take
in.

DIFFICULTY WITH PERPETUAL

THOUGHT

If caffeine makes you
nervous or jittery, you
might want to cut back.
Instead of coffee or
energy drinks, try
decaffeinated coffee,
herbal tea, or water.

Everything that is been occupying your thoughts

Although coffee offers health advantages in moderation, consumption should not exceed 400 mg per day, or 4–5 cups (0.9–1.2 L).

However, caffeine
sensitive persons may
suffer more anxiety and
tension after taking less
caffeine, so evaluate
your tolerance.

Having friends and family
around may help you deal
with worry and get
through tough times.

FINAL ARTICLE!

In a 2019 research of 163
Latinx college-age young
people, lesser support
from friends, family, and
romantic partners was
linked to loneliness,
depression, and stress.

DAY 6 OF EMBRACING CHANGE

A STATE OF MIND THAT COULD TRANSFORM

There is a correlation between having a social support system and having better mental health overall.

Practical Steps You Can Do Right Now

When you are feeling alone and do not have relatives or friends on whom you can rely, social support groups may be able to assist you.

DIFFICULTY WITH PERPETUAL

THOUGHT

You may want to think
about becoming a member
of a sports team or club,
or volunteering for a
cause that is important
to you.

Everything that is been
occupying your thoughts

Only certain pressures
are within your control.
Too much on your plate
may raise stress and
reduce self-care time.

Increasing the frequency
with which you use the
word "no" might be one
method to assist decrease
stress and maintain your
mental health.

This is especially true if you take on more than you can handle, since having a lot of duties may make you feel stressed.

FINAL ARTICLE!

You can feel less stressed if you are careful about what you take on and say "no" to things that will add to your workload without being necessary.

DAY SEVEN OF YOUR JOURNEY TO TRANSFORMATION

A STATE OF MIND THAT COULD TRANSFORM

Setting limits, especially with people who make you feel stressed, is a good way to look out for your health.

Practical Steps You Can Do Right Now

This can be as easy as telling a family member or friend not to drop by without warning or breaking plans with a friend if you need more space.

DIFFICULTY WITH PERPETUAL

THOUGHT

Keeping up with your to-do list and not putting things off when you're not stressed is another way to deal with your stress.

Everything that is been occupying your thoughts

Procrastination may lower productivity and put you behind. Stress may harm your health and sleep.

It's also true that you might put things off more when you're stressed as a way to deal with it.

A study of 140 medicine students in China found a link between putting things off and feeling more stressed.

FINAL ARTICLE!

The study also found links between putting things off and taking longer to respond to stress and harsher parenting styles, such as punishing and rejecting children.

WELL DONE!

IT GIVES US GREAT PLEASURE
TO KNOW THAT YOU HAVE
REACHED THE CONCLUSION OF
THIS MANUAL.

EMBRACE WHAT YOU HAVE
LEARNED AND DO NOT LET IT
SLIP YOUR MIND.

DONATING COPIES IS A GREAT
WAY TO SHOW THAT YOU CARE
BY ALLOWING OTHERS TO
IMPROVE THEIR LIFE AS WELL.

Made in United States
Orlando, FL
20 September 2024

51748432R00026